CLOUD TECTONICS

José Rivera

BROADWAY PLAY PUBLISHING INC
224 E 62nd St, NY NY 10065
212 772-8334 fax: 212 772-8358
BroadwayPlayPub.com

CLOUD TECTONICS
© Copyright 1997 by José Rivera

First printing: June 1997
This printing: February 2012
I S B N: 978-0-88145-137-5

Book design: Marie Donovan
Page make-up: Adobe Indesign
Copy editing: Liam Brosnahan
Printed and bound in the U S A

ABOUT THE AUTHOR

José Rivera is a recipient of two OBIE Awards for Playwriting (for MARISOL and REFERENCES TO SALVADOR DALI MAKE ME HOT, both at The Joseph Papp Public Theater), a Fulbright Arts Fellowship, a Whiting Foundation Award, a McKnight Fellowship, and a 2005 Impact Award. He studied with Gabriel García Márquez at Sundance and was writer-in-residence at the Royal Court Theater, London.

U S theater productions include THE HOUSE OF RAMON IGLESIA (Ensemble Studio Theater, American Playhouse), MARISOL (Humana Festival, La Jolla Playhouse, Hartford Stage Co), CLOUD TECTONICS (Humana Festival, Playwrights Horizons, Goodman Theater), REFERENCES TO SALVADOR DALI MAKE ME HOT (South Coast Rep), EACH DAY DIES WITH SLEEP (Circle Rep, Berkeley Rep), SONNETS FOR AN OLD CENTURY (Nuyorican Poets Cafe), SUEÑO (Hartford Stage, Manhattan Class Company, Milwaukee Rep), GIANTS HAVE US IN THEIR BOOKS (Magic Theater, INTAR Theater), MARICELA DE LA LUZ LIGHTS THE WORLD (La Jolla Playhouse), THE PROMISE (Ensemble Studio Theater, Los Angeles Theater Center), THE STREET OF THE SUN (Mark Taper Forum), ADORATION OF THE OLD WOMAN (La Jolla Playhouse), SCHOOL OF THE AMERICAS (Joseph Papp Public Theater and

LAByrinth Theater), MASSACRE (SING TO YOUR CHILDREN) (Goodman Theater and Teatro Vista), BRAINPEOPLE (A C T, San Francisco), BOLEROS FOR THE DISENCHANTED (Yale Rep, Huntington Stage, A C T, Goodman Theater), HUMAN EMOTIONAL PROCESS (commission at the McCarter Theater), and HOURS ARE FEMININE. His work has been seen in Puerto Rico, London, Paris, Edinburgh, Mexico City, Singapore, Greece, Sweden, Norway, Canada, Peru, Australia, Germany, Romania, and the Philippines.

The screenplay for his first produced film *The Motorcycle Diaries* (Walter Salles, director) was nominated for a 2005 Academy Award for Best Adapted Screenplay, a BAFTA Award, and a Writers Guild Award, and received Spain's Goya Award for Best Adapted Screenplay as well as Argentina's top screenwriting award. For television he co-created and produced the series *Eerie, Indiana* (N B C). He has written screen adaptations of Kerouac's *On The Road* (Francis Ford Coppola, producer, Walter Salles, director), *Three Apples Fell From Heaven* (Door/Key Productions), and the novels *The Brief Wondrous Life of Oscar Wao* and *American Rust. Celestina*, a film based on CLOUD TECTONICS, will mark his debut as a feature film director.

Rivera is a member of The LAByrinth Theater Company, The Ensemble Studio Theater, and the Lark Theater Playwrights Workshop.

CLOUD TECTONICS received its world premiere at the 19th Annual Humana Festival of New American Plays at the Actors Theatre of Louisville (Jon Jory, Producing Director), in Louisville, Kentucky, in March 1995. The cast and creative contributors were as follows:

CELESTINA DEL SOL .... Camilia Sanes
ANIBAL DE LA LUNA .... Robert Montano
NELSON DE LA LUNA .... Javi Mulero

Director .... Tina Landau
Set design .... Paul Owen
Costume design .... Laura Patterson
Lighting design .... T J Gerckens
Sound design .... Martin J Bissonnette
Fight director .... Drew Fracher
Stage manager .... Michele Streckler
Assistant stage manager .... Janette L Hubert
Dramaturg .... Michele Volansky

CLOUD TECTONICS was produced by the La Jolla Playhouse (Michael Greif, Artistic Director; Terence Dwyer, Managing Director; Robert Blacker, Associate Artistic Director) on 20 June 1995. The cast was as follows:

CELESTINA DEL SOL .... Camilia Sanes
ANIBAL DE LA LUNA .... Luis Antonio Ramos
NELSON DE LA LUNA .... Javi Mulero

Director .... Tina Landau
Set design .... Riccardo Hernandez
Costume design .... Brandin Baron
Lighting design .... Anna Militello
Sound design .... Mark Bennett
Dramaturg .... Gregory Gunter
Stage manager .... Kristen Harris

CHARACTERS & SETTING

CELESTINA DEL SOL, *twenties*
ANIBAL DE LA LUNA, *thirties*
NELSON DE LA LUNA, *twenties*

SCENES

PROLOGUE: *Los Angeles. The present. Night.*
CLOUD TECTONICS: *Same. Later that night.*
EPILOGUE: *Same. Forty years later.*

There is no intermission.

Special thanks to Ivonne Coll for the Spanish translation of
CELESTINA's *speech.*

Ah dejame recordate como eras entonces, cuando aun no existias.
Pablo Neruda

...love was the promised land, an ark on which two might escape the Flood.
Julian Barnes, *A History of the World in 10 1/2 Chapters*

The mystery of what a couple is, exactly, is almost the only true mystery left to us, and when we come to the end of it there will be no more need for literature....
Mavis Gallant

...the discovery that the speed of light appeared the same to every observer, no matter how he was moving, led to the theory of relativity—and in that one had to abandon the idea that there was a unique and absolute time.
Stephen W Hawking, *A Brief History of Time*

Todo me parece como un sueño todavia....
Danny Daniel

for Heather

PROLOGUE

(*Los Angeles. Night. A bare stage with:*)

(*A floating bed, high in the air, tilted so the upstage headboard is slightly higher than the downstage footboard.*)

(*A glass wall. Water drips down the side of the glass wall. It represents a city bus stop during a rainstorm.*)

(*A pair of microphones on C-stands, downstage, a few feet apart.*)

(*The Prologue begins with bolero music: Los Panchos singing* Por El Amor De Una Mujer.)

(CELESTINA DEL SOL *is standing at the bus stop. There's the sound of rain.* CELESTINA *is soaking wet. She carries a small shopping bag. She wears a thin maternity dress and she shivers. She looks exhausted, as if she's been wandering on foot for days. It's impossible to tell her actual age. It's impossible to tell if she's rich or poor. She's very, very pregnant.*)

(*As the bolero plays,* CELESTINA *holds her thumb out, hoping to catch a ride, but there doesn't seem to be any traffic in Los Angeles tonight. She reaches into a pocket, pulls out some saltine crackers, and eats them hungrily, savoring each bite.*)

(*Car lights wash over* CELESTINA. *She sticks her thumb up higher. The lights cruise past her and disappear. Disappointed,* CELESTINA *eats another cracker.*)

(*We wait for the bolero to end or fade out.*)

(A moment's silence, then another car's headlights pass over CELESTINA. *They stay on her. She holds her thumb up expectantly. The car's horn beckons her and she happily leaves the wall and goes to one of the microphones.)*

(The microphones are suddenly awash in red light.)

*(*ANIBAL DE LA LUNA *enters and goes to the other microphone.* ANIBAL *is a pleasant-looking man, thirties, dressed in an American Airlines ground crew uniform.* ANIBAL *and* CELESTINA *perform the following scene into the microphones. At no time do they pantomime being in a car.)*

(During the Prologue, ANIBAL's *house in the Echo Park section of Los Angeles is loaded in.)*

CELESTINA: *(Shivering)* Thank you so much for this.

ANIBAL: Jesus, you're soaked. There's a jacket in the backseat.

CELESTINA: *(Putting on jacket)* Thank you.

(Short beat)

ANIBAL: I can't believe anyone's out in that deluge. They're calling it the storm of the century.

CELESTINA: Where am I?

ANIBAL: Los Angeles.

CELESTINA: *(Troubled)* Los Angeles?

ANIBAL: Corner of Virgil and Santa Monica.

CELESTINA: *(Means nothing to her)* Oh.

*(*CELESTINA *says no more. She rubs her pregnant stomach and stares ahead. Her silence makes* ANIBAL *a little nervous.)*

ANIBAL: Can you believe this rain for L A? *Coño!* Raging floods on Fairfax...bodies floating down the L A River...L A X closed...if the Big One came right

now, forget it, half this city would die. But that's L A
for you: disasters just waiting to happen.

(ANIBAL *laughs. No response from* CELESTINA.)

ANIBAL: I lived in New York. Lived in every borough
except Staten Island. And Brooklyn. And Queens. And
the thing is, New York kills its people one-by-one, you
know? A gun here, a knife there, hand-to-hand combat
at the A T M, little countable deaths. But this? This
L A thing? We're talking mass death, mass destruction.
One freak flood at the wrong time of year and
hundreds die...the atmosphere sags from its own toxic
heaviness and thousands perish...the Big One is finally
born and eats a hundred thousand souls for breakfast.
And I'm not even talking fire season!

(CELESTINA *looks at* ANIBAL *for the first time.*)

CELESTINA: Why don't you go back to New York?

ANIBAL: Are you kidding? I love it here. I have a house
here. I have gorgeous fucking incredible-looking
women falling outta the sky here! *Coño,* I've made a
commitment to that!

(*No response from* CELESTINA. *She eats a cracker quietly,
her mind far away.* ANIBAL *looks at her a long moment.*)

ANIBAL: You alright?

CELESTINA: The trucker that dropped me off kept
touching my knees and I screamed.

ANIBAL: How long were you out there?

CELESTINA: I don't know.

ANIBAL: You don't know?

CELESTINA: I don't have a watch...I don't keep a
watch...I don't keep "time".... "Time" and I don't hang
out together!

ANIBAL: (*Not understanding*) Oh. Where can I take you?

CELESTINA: I don't know.

ANIBAL: Where were you hitching to?

CELESTINA: Nowhere. I'm not going anywhere. I don't know where I'm going, I'm sorry.

ANIBAL: You're just out there hitching? In a hurricane? Pregnant? For fun?

CELESTINA: Are you going to ask me a lot of questions?

ANIBAL: Why don't I take you to a hospital? Get someone to check out your baby.

CELESTINA: No! No! Don't do that! I don't want doctors asking me a lot of questions!

ANIBAL: Maybe the police could....

CELESTINA: No police! Please! No police! I don't want to go to the police!

ANIBAL: No friends or family in L A?

CELESTINA: No one. I have no one. You're the only one I have!

ANIBAL: *(Choosing to ignore that)* Well, you're in my car, I gotta take you somewhere....

CELESTINA: Take me to this baby's father. I'm looking for this baby's father. His name is Rodrigo Cruz. Do you know him? He's a very handsome and dishonest man.

ANIBAL: No, I don't think I....

CELESTINA: Nobody knows him. I ask everybody. That trucker took me to every state looking for Rodrigo Cruz!

ANIBAL: ...I'm sorry....

CELESTINA: I started my journey on Montauk Point: a room in a house, very small, my Papi sailed boats for tourists, it was some distance back—but I—I lost all track of "time" —I hate to use that word— "time" — but it's the only word I have, isn't it?

ANIBAL: *Coño,* I'm not following this....

CELESTINA: I can give you details of Rodrigo Cruz. He worked for Papi repairing the boat. His eyes were ocean-green. His back was wrinkled. But I can't tell you when he was like that, okay? He might have changed, you see? I can't tell you his age. Do you know how hard it is to find someone when you can't tell anyone their age?

ANIBAL: Well, it's not a problem I ever....

CELESTINA: All this traveling has been a blur! It's a huge country! I never should have left my house in Montauk! I was safe in my house! Papi and Mami had it all worked out for me! They took away all the clocks!

ANIBAL: *(Completely lost)* The clocks?

CELESTINA: But I was sleeping when that gorgeous son-of-a-bitch Rodrigo Cruz came into my room! He knocked me up! He left! Now look at me! I'm starving and lost and sick of these soggy FUCKING crackers... and I'm just so tired of being pregnant!

ANIBAL: *(Worried)* Take it easy...

CELESTINA: You can let me out right here, I'm sorry!

ANIBAL: But we haven't moved. Light's still red.

CELESTINA: *(Looking)* Oh. Right.

(CELESTINA wants to cry. ANIBAL looks at her.)

ANIBAL: You all right?

CELESTINA: Please, I don't want to bother you anymore.

ANIBAL: I don't want you sleeping outside. Not with a baby coming.

CELESTINA: I've done it before!

(The relentless rain slaps the car as ANIBAL *contemplates his options.)*

ANIBAL: *Coño,* okay, listen: if you promise me you're not an axe-murderer...I promise you I'm not an axe-murderer too, okay? You can stay in my house tonight, okay? Just tonight, okay? I'm right up here in Echo Park, okay?

CELESTINA: I can? I can't.

ANIBAL: I promise not to touch your knees, okay?

*(*CELESTINA *looks at* ANIBAL.*)*

CELESTINA: What's your name?

ANIBAL: Oh I'm sorry. Anibal de la Luna. Nice to meet you.

CELESTINA: I'm Celestina del Sol.

(She reaches out her hand. ANIBAL *and* CELESTINA *shake hands. She smiles.)*

CELESTINA: Okay. Let's go to your place.

(The light turns green.)

(The lights go down on ANIBAL *and* CELESTINA. *The crew finishes assembling* ANIBAL's *house.* ANIBAL *and* CELESTINA *exit.)*

(The microphones are struck.)

END OF PROLOGUE

CLOUD TECTONICS

(The lights are dark in ANIBAL'*s house, a modest 1915 Craftsman house, working class, not Hollywood.)*

(The living room, kitchen, and small eating area are basically one room full of sentimental family pictures, and second- and third-hand furniture. The door in the living room leads to the front porch. Another door leads to the bathroom.)

(There are a couple of subtle plaster cracks on the walls from a recent earthquake.)

(Everything—sink, television, stereo, refrigerator, microwave, V C R, telephone, O'Keefe & Merrit stove, etc.—should be fully functional. There's a Sparkletts water dispenser in the kitchen: the bottle is empty.)

(The only light in the house comes from the glowing digital clocks on all the appliances. It's 8:05 P M.)

(The glass wall has been incorporated into the house. Two ladders have been placed next to the floating bed to make it accessible to the living room.)

(We hear footsteps. The sound of keys unlocking the front door. The door opens. Suddenly all the digital clocks turn off and come back on blinking a new time: 12:00. It stays 12:00 for the rest of the scene.)

*(*CELESTINA *and* ANIBAL *enter from the porch. Both are dripping wet.* CELESTINA *now wears a thin suede jacket.* ANIBAL *carries in a five-gallon bottle of Sparkletts water.)*

(With the door wide open we hear distant police, ambulance, and fire truck sirens. CELESTINA *closes the door and the sirens stop.)*

ANIBAL: Watch your step.

CELESTINA: It's a pretty house.

ANIBAL: It's a craftsman. Built in 1915.

CELESTINA: Is that old?

ANIBAL: In L A it's the Middle Ages.

CELESTINA: *(Not understanding)* Oh.

(ANIBAL *puts the water bottle on the kitchen floor as* CELESTINA *takes off the wet jacket. They both take off their water-logged shoes.)*

ANIBAL: *(Re: her shoes)* Just leave them anywhere.

CELESTINA: *(Looking around, smiles)* I'll never forget this as long as I live.

ANIBAL: Let me turn up the heat. Get some light going here.

(ANIBAL *turns up the heat and turns on some lights.)*

(ANIBAL *looks over at* CELESTINA—*getting his first full view of her. She's much more pregnant, and much more beautiful, than he realized. She smiles warmly at him.)*

CELESTINA: You have the most beautiful house, Anibal.

ANIBAL: It's dry at least. More than I can say for you.

(ANIBAL *goes to the bathroom and comes back with a towel, which he tosses to* CELESTINA. *She dries her face, arms, and feet.)*

CELESTINA: You're the kindest, most beautiful man in the world! And this is the happiest night of my life!

ANIBAL: *(Smiles)* Can I get you anything to drink?

CELESTINA: *(Eager)* Water. Please.

(ANIBAL *goes to the kitchen.*)

ANIBAL: So please make yourself at home. Sit. Relax.

(ANIBAL *puts the full Sparkletts bottle on the dispenser. He takes the empty bottle out to the porch: again, as he opens the door, we hear distant sirens which stop when he closes the door.*)

(*Too happy to sit still,* CELESTINA *starts exploring the house, checking out pictures on tables, books on bookshelves, etc.*)

CELESTINA: Everything is so beautiful. Everything in order.

ANIBAL: Debbie does that.

CELESTINA: My little room in Montauk had no order. It wasn't big, but it was my whole world. Things were everywhere, on top of everything: I'd sleep in my clothes, and eat in bed, and read detective novels, hardly ever sleep, dream wide awake, make plans that were never fulfilled, watch storms coming in, the moon's neurotic phases, hear stars being scraped across the sky, dance, sing *boleros*, make love to myself over and over, live a whole life in one room! (*She laughs as she holds herself and does a little dance around the room.*)

ANIBAL: (*Giving her a look*) You want a quesadilla?

CELESTINA: And my Mami and Papi worked so hard for me. They loved me so much. They thought I was cursed! They really did! They put everything in its proper place for me!

(ANIBAL *looks at* CELESTINA *a long moment, not sure what to make of all this.*)

ANIBAL: Your parents thought you were cursed?

CELESTINA: Yeah. They're dead. I'd love a quesadilla.

ANIBAL: Wait.

CELESTINA: Papi used to cross himself when he looked at me. Mami wouldn't breast feed me. They kept eighteen statues of Jesus Christ in my room!

ANIBAL: Wait. Why did you live in one room...?

(CELESTINA *looks at* ANIBAL, *aware of his look. She laughs.*)

CELESTINA: I hope I don't sound...I hope I don't sound...I'm not a lunatic. Hey. You're in no danger, stranger. It's just hard for me to tell a story. Straight.

ANIBAL: *(Worried; re: her baby)* Just take it easy. For both of you.

CELESTINA: *(Touching her stomach)* This baby must think I'm a lunatic too!

ANIBAL: But I don't—.

CELESTINA: I wonder what this baby hears. Oh God! This baby must've heard me talking to that trucker, and all his dirty words! Ugly, filthy man!

(CELESTINA *suddenly gets a fierce contraction that doubles her over.* ANIBAL *goes to her and takes her hand.*)

ANIBAL: Celestina, please...if you...if you sat down, I'd feel a lot better...

CELESTINA: *(Pain)* Why?

ANIBAL: 'Cause if you get too agitated, you might...I mean, I don't want you having that baby all over my floor tonight....

CELESTINA: And your floor is so clean!

ANIBAL: Yes...I mean, you're not, like, *coño*, due tonight, are you?

CELESTINA: *(Pain subsiding)* I don't know.

ANIBAL: You don't know?

(*The discomfort goes away and* CELESTINA *straightens up again. She smiles as if nothing happened.*)

CELESTINA: I don't think so.

ANIBAL: Well, wait. How pregnant are you? Exactly.

CELESTINA: *(Defensive)* What do you mean?

ANIBAL: How far along are you?

CELESTINA: I'm not really sure.

ANIBAL: You're not sure?

CELESTINA: This is the warmest, most enchanting house I've ever....

ANIBAL: Wait. Isn't knowing how pregnant you are...a little basic? Like knowing your age?

CELESTINA: Yes...yes it is...but you should never ask a woman's age, you might not like what you hear! *(Smiles at him)* Can I have my water?

(ANIBAL looks at CELESTINA—then goes to the Sparkletts dispenser and pours CELESTINA a tall glass of water. He gives it to her.)

(CELESTINA drinks the water very fast, almost choking on it, like she hasn't had water in a long time. Finished, she holds out her empty glass for more.)

(As ANIBAL takes CELESTINA's empty glass and goes back for a refill, CELESTINA finds a framed picture of a young woman on a table.)

CELESTINA: So do you have a lot of "gorgeous fucking incredible-looking women" in your life, Anibal?

(ANIBAL hands CELESTINA the glass of water.)

ANIBAL: *(Re: photograph)* Well, no. Well, one. That one.

CELESTINA: She's beautiful.

ANIBAL: That's Debbie.

(CELESTINA looks at the photograph a long time. ANIBAL waits for her to say something.)

ANIBAL: She's at her office now. She sleeps there a lot. She works for Disney. She answers phones. She's gorgeous. She's Puerto Rican too but she changed her name from Epifania Niguayona Gonzalez to Debbie Shapiro. They still don't respect her. She thinks they do. But she's deluding herself. I can tell. I know guys. I know when a guy is thinking pussy and every guy she works with at Disney is thinking pussy. She thinks they're thinking brain cells. They're not going to make her an executive like she thinks. She's going to remain a receptionist until she turns thirty, then they're gonna fire her and get a younger, prettier, whiter-looking Latin girl to replace her.

CELESTINA: Will she mind my being here?

ANIBAL: She'd hate it except you're pregnant. Deb doesn't believe in friendship between the sexes, she believes in sex between the sexes. Being pregnant makes you safe.

CELESTINA: *(Surprised)* I'm safe?

ANIBAL: Guess so.

(CELESTINA *puts the photograph down, finishes her glass of water, and looks at* ANIBAL.)

CELESTINA: What do you believe? Sex or friendship?

ANIBAL: I believe friendship between the sexes is not only possible, it's preferable. Makes everything cleaner. But then I don't work in the movie business. I load luggage at L A X. There's no sex in that job.

CELESTINA: *(Shocked)* None?

(Beat. ANIBAL *isn't sure how far he wants this conversation to go, but there's something about* CELESTINA. *He can't help but open up to her.)*

ANIBAL: The closest is...I look up at an airplane sometimes and it's full of people going to New York

and sometimes I make eye contact with a woman
at a windowseat in First Class. And she's looking
down at me, daydreaming, maybe she's afraid of the
flight, thinking this could be her last hour on earth,
wondering if she's done enough, dared enough, eaten
enough, and everyone around her seems dead already.
And that fear of crashing is bringing all her latent
sexual dreams up from their deep well, and she's
getting all excited by her own images—and there we
are, making split-second eye contact and suddenly that
faceless male in her dreamworld has a pair of eyes...
and they are vivid eyes, and they are Puerto Rican
eyes, and they are my eyes, Celestina.

(A short silence. CELESTINA *goes to* ANIBAL. *She gets close
to him—so close her huge belly gently touches his stomach.
She looks into* ANIBAL's *eyes. The intensity of this makes*
ANIBAL *a little nervous.)*

ANIBAL: What are you doing?

CELESTINA: Can I see?

ANIBAL: Can you see? What? Can you what?

CELESTINA: Your vivid, Puerto Rican eyes, Anibal, can I
see them?

ANIBAL: *(Nervous)* Why? No.

CELESTINA: Just because. Let me.

ANIBAL: *Coño,* I brought you here on faith, now. That
you're not a killer. Not a psycho. Not a hypnotizing,
blood-drinking Scientologist...

*(*CELESTINA *looks deep into* ANIBAL's *eyes.)*

CELESTINA: I think about sex all the time, though I've
only had one lover in my life, only one time. Rodrigo
Cruz. And I almost had two! That despicable trucker
who kept touching my knees. But I ran away from him.
I took my chances in the rain. But even he couldn't

stop my endless daydreaming and nightdreaming
about sex: about Rodrigo's wrinkled back, my legs
wrapped around his face...this obsession of mine...this
tidal wave that started sometime when I was younger,
when I lived in that one room. When Papi bought me
a bicycle to give me something else to think about
besides my body, and one glorious day I was allowed
to ride around and around the house, because my Papi
wanted me to count numbers, count numbers, over
and over; he said it would teach me about the nature
of "time," and I tried and tried, I really did, but I didn't
learn anything, I was just so grateful to be outside my
little room for once!

(Beat) Then Papi hired Rodrigo to work on his boat
"The Celestina." And I would stare at him from my
window as he worked. He was beautiful. I wondered
if I was in love. Is that what it felt like? And he would
look back at me and stare and his hair was so long and
black. And I wondered is that what love looks like?
And I don't know how many years passed... (I didn't
know the word "years" then. I learned it on the road
when the trucker taught me all kinds of words like
"years" and "now" and "yesterday" and "minute"
and "century") ...and it must have been years...
because years are longer than days (I learned this!)...
and Rodrigo's hair was long and grey and he snuck
into my room and did his dirty thing and left me...and
my parents died in the other room and I went out to
see because the house had grown so quiet and there
they were in their little bed, holding hands, the green
bedspread half covering their wrinkled bodies, they
were naked and pale and covered in long grey hairs
and very, very dead. That's the one time I stopped
dreaming of sex when I called the police and told them
Mami and Papi were dead, then I got dressed, and I
lost all track of "time" and I got scared, and I ran out
into the rain because I was sure they'd blame me and

in my endless stay in my one room I didn't learn much, but I learned by reading detective novels that when somebody dies the police always come to take you away and kill you with a lightning chair. That's when I hit the road, pregnant, looking for Rodrigo Cruz, angry and excited because he was the only man I ever had sex with and I keep thinking about sex with Rodrigo and I love the word sex and if I could fuck fuck fuck all day I would!

(ANIBAL *impulsively, quickly kisses* CELESTINA. *She gasps. He turns away.*)

ANIBAL: Let me start those quesadillas for you!

(ANIBAL *quickly turns on the griddle and busies himself in the kitchen.*)

CELESTINA: I should leave. (*She starts to go to the front door.*)

ANIBAL: I don't want you to leave.

CELESTINA: You don't think I'm strange?

ANIBAL: I do think you're strange. But I don't want you to leave.

CELESTINA: But I don't know how long I've been here. I don't know if it's been too long! I should go!

ANIBAL: (*Re: the kiss*) I'm sorry I did that! I never do that!

CELESTINA: Have I been here minutes? Days?! Shit! I knew this would happen!

ANIBAL: A half hour at the most! Twenty minutes. Not days.

CELESTINA: Are you sure?

(ANIBAL *looks at his watch.*)

ANIBAL: My watch stopped.

CELESTINA: *(Knew this would happen)* I really have to go before Rodrigo turns into an unrecognizable old man and dies!

(ANIBAL *looks at all the digital clocks in house—all are blinking 12:00.)*

ANIBAL: The clocks have stopped....

(CELESTINA *goes to put on her shoes and the wet jacket.)*

CELESTINA: I can't miss my chance to make that bastard do right by me!

(CELESTINA *goes to the door, opens it. We hear sirens.)*

(ANIBAL *grabs* CELESTINA's *arm, physically stopping her from running out.)*

ANIBAL: Celestina, wait a second—.

CELESTINA: I can't wait a second; I don't know what you mean!

ANIBAL: I can't let you go out into a fucking typhoon—.

CELESTINA: But—

ANIBAL: You've been here only a few minutes. Just minutes. Tomorrow morning, when the sun comes up, it'll be only a few hours....

(Beat. CELESTINA *looks at* ANIBAL.*)*

CELESTINA: Hours? Is it a lot? Is it long?

ANIBAL: *Coño*...I think you're...I think something has happened to you, Celestina, something really bad, I don't know what, but it's some kind of trauma, and you're not making any sense....

CELESTINA: *(Offended)* I have not lost my mind.

ANIBAL: Please, just stay a little longer, okay? Eat dinner. Sleep on the sofabed. In the morning, we'll have a big breakfast and I'll give you some money. Drive you wherever you want, okay?

(ANIBAL *goes to the kitchen and comes back with another glass of water. He holds it out for* CELESTINA. *Still thirsty,* CELESTINA *comes back in and takes the glass of water.*)

CELESTINA: Your beauty is overwhelming, Anibal.

(ANIBAL *closes the door. The sirens stop.* CELESTINA *takes off her shoes and the jacket.*)

(*Keeping a watchful eye on* CELESTINA *as she drinks the water,* ANIBAL *goes to the kitchen, opens the refrigerator, and takes out packets of tortillas, cheese, salsa, and guacamole. As he prepares dinner, he can't help but looking at her in wonder.*)

ANIBAL: Who are you, Celestina?

(CELESTINA *smiles at the inevitable question, then thinks a moment. She starts setting the table for dinner as* ANIBAL *puts the tortillas and cheese on the hot griddle.*)

CELESTINA: How do you know what "time" feels like, Anibal?

(ANIBAL *looks at her a second.*)

CELESTINA: In your body? You feel it, don't you? Pushing at your heart muscles. Pricking the nerves in your brain. Turning some on, turning some off. Is that what "time" feels like? And where is "time"? Is the organ for "time" the heart? Is it the spinal chord, that silver waterfall of nerves and memories: is "time" in there? Is it the gonads? Does "time" have a sound? What bells, Anibal, what vibrating string played by what virtuoso accompanies the passage of "time"? Is "time" blue? Does it taste like steak? Can you fuck it? Or is it just the invisible freight train that runs you over every single day...breaking you into smaller and smaller pieces...pieces so small they can't hold your soul to the earth anymore, and that's why you die? C'mon, Anibal, help me out here!

ANIBAL: We just know. Common sense tells us.

CELESTINA: Well, then...what if there are people born who don't have that sense? Don't have that inner clock telling them when a moment has passed, when another has started, how a day feels different from a year. What would you say to such people?

ANIBAL: *Coño*: your imagination....

CELESTINA: And what if these people, because their inner clocks are broken, or they were never born with one to begin with, what if these people don't progress through space and "time" the same way you do? They don't age smoothly. They stay little far longer than they should. Then, all of a sudden, they change into an old person overnight? Or the rhythms of the day mean nothing. So they sleep for weeks at a "time." They stay awake all winter scaring the shit out of their parents! They can make love for two weeks straight without a break!

ANIBAL: I don't know.

(Beat)

CELESTINA: No. Of course not. How could you?

(Dinner is ready. The table is set. CELESTINA *looks at the table appreciatively.)*

CELESTINA: I should wash my hands.

ANIBAL: *(Re: bathroom)* That way.

*(*CELESTINA *starts to go off. Then she looks at* ANIBAL. *She goes to him, kisses him on the cheek, and embraces him. He holds her close.)*

CELESTINA: Papi told me he was twenty-five when I was born. Before he died, we celebrated his seventy-seventh birthday. When the trucker picked me up outside of Montauk Point, I was pregnant and starting to show. When we crossed the frontier into Los Angeles, before he touched my knees, he put two

candles on a little cake and said we were celebrating
two years together. *(Beat)* So that's who I am: I'm
a fifty-four year old woman, Anibal, and I've been
pregnant with this baby for two years.

(CELESTINA goes to the bathroom and closes the door.)

*(ANIBAL is alone. He goes to the telephone in the living
room. Picks it up. It's dead. He slams it.)*

ANIBAL: Shit.

*(ANIBAL goes to the T V and turns it on. All he can get, in
channel after channel, is static. He turns on a radio. More
static.)*

(ANIBAL goes back to the kitchen and hides all the knives.)

*(There's a knock at the door. ANIBAL looks at the door,
worried. A second knock. ANIBAL goes to the door and opens
it. Sirens.)*

*(ANIBAL's younger brother, Sergeant NELSON DE LA
LUNA, is there. NELSON is taller, broader than his older
brother: he has a sweet baby face, short hair, and a little
mustache. NELSON wears an army issue raincoat and army
boots.)*

ANIBAL: Nelson?

NELSON: *(Big smile)* Brother!

*(NELSON laughs and scoops up ANIBAL in a big bear hug.
The brothers kiss and pound each others' backs.)*

ANIBAL: Son-of-a-bitch, Nelson, what the fuck are you
doing here?!

NELSON: Surprise! Nice house!

*(NELSON comes in, takes off his rain coat. Underneath he
wears army issue t-shirt, khakis, dog tags, etc. ANIBAL still
can't believe his brother's there. He closes the door. Sirens
stop.)*

ANIBAL: Look at you. Fucking amazing. Are you alone?

NELSON: No, I got half the company out in the Grand National, asshole. Man look at you. You old.

ANIBAL: Fuck you too. What an asshole; you didn't even call me....

NELSON: Surprise, surprise, how much you pay for this dump?

ANIBAL: What a dickhead! So what's up? I thought you were in Germany.

NELSON: Not any more, bro. They shipped my ass to Fort Benning, Georgia, six months ago. Then they sent my ass out here for two days.

ANIBAL: Are you in training for something? Getting ready to invade some hapless third world country?

NELSON: "Hapless." What a homo. You got a beer? *(He goes to the refrigerator and helps himself to a beer.)*

ANIBAL: Have a beer.

NELSON: I'm fucking out in Death Valley now. It's a fucking lake. I thought you lived in sunny Southern California, jerk-off.

ANIBAL: It rains out here too, asswipe. *Coño*, it's great to see you, Nelson.

(They embrace exuberantly again, pound backs.)

NELSON: So yeah, got my ass shipped to Death Valley, I'm good to go, bro, desert training for the Middle East or some towelhead shithole with oil underneath it...fucking tanks all over the place, blow up anything stupid enough to get in our way—mostly stray sheep and coyotes— 'cause we're men, Anibal, not pussies like you: men, MEN!

ANIBAL: *(Laughs)* Get outta my face with that shit.

NELSON: Yo, it beats jerkin' off all day like you, so this is your house finally, I gotta get me one of these, I

guess loading luggage really pays, what: you helpin'
smuggle drugs-n-shit?

ANIBAL: *(Laughs)* How long are you staying?

NELSON: Man, I'm hosed. I gotta be back in Death
Valley oh-five-hundred tomorrow morning for a
fucking dipshit meeting with my C O that's only
supposed to last five minutes. So I can only hang 'bout
an hour, 'cause the roads suck tonight.

ANIBAL: *(Disappointed)* An hour? Nelson, I haven't seen
you in six years.

NELSON: Time flies, motherfucker!

ANIBAL: So why can't you call the guy—?

NELSON: No way. Gotta be there. They gotta see my ass
in front of the C O, in person. It's really fucking stupid.

ANIBAL: The army's perfect for you.

NELSON: *(Re: ANIBAL)* What a waste of a human being.
Man, you get uglier and stupider all the time.

ANIBAL: You're just pissed my mother loved me and
she didn't love you.

(NELSON starts looking for the bathroom.)

NELSON: Aw shit, where's the head, man? All I've
eaten is beef jerky and I gotta take a massive dump.

ANIBAL: You're a poet, Nelson, you know that? A poet
of our time.

NELSON: Yo, eat me!

ANIBAL: There's somebody in the bathroom. A woman.

NELSON: *(Surprised)* You got a woman in your
bathroom, Anibal?

ANIBAL: Her name is Celestina. I picked her up tonight.

NELSON: *(Big smile)* Brother! You're not a total waste!

(NELSON high-fives ANIBAL.)

ANIBAL: No, she's pregnant, Nelson, and she's...I think...mentally disturbed or something...or she's living in a dreamworld, I don't know.

NELSON: Women.

ANIBAL: She looks like she's twenty-five years old but she says she's fifty-four.

NELSON: That's fucking L A, bro.

ANIBAL: And she says she's been pregnant for two years.

NELSON: And you picked her up? You're not an asshole!

ANIBAL: She was hitching. In this storm. I can't drive by somebody like that.

NELSON: A total fairy. What a liberal. Is she cute?

ANIBAL: She's gorgeous.

NELSON: Oh well, that's cool. I could fuck an insane pregnant girl if she's gorgeous.

ANIBAL: Don't be a pig, Nelson—.

NELSON: What? I'll have that bitch howlin' at the moon!

ANIBAL: She's not—.

NELSON: Hey, I've been in a tank nine weeks, bro, I'm ready to seduce goats. Swear: my mother must've been exposed to radiation when you were born.

ANIBAL: *(Laughs)* Fuck you through the head.

NELSON: You're the fucking poet of our time! Asshole! Liberal! I'mma fuckin' bodyslam you!

(NELSON *lunges at* ANIBAL. ANIBAL *fights him off. They wrestle around the living room, knocking furniture around, laughing.* NELSON *catches* ANIBAL.)

(NELSON *lifts* ANIBAL *and prepares to bodyslam him.*)

ANIBAL: NELSON—DOOOOOOON'T!!

(CELESTINA *comes in. She's got a gun. She aims it at* NELSON*'s head. Both men freeze.*)

NELSON: Oh shit.

ANIBAL: Celestina...?

NELSON: *(Already admiring her)* Training and instinct tell me that's a gun.

CELESTINA: Put him down.

(NELSON *quickly puts* ANIBAL *down.* CELESTINA *continues pointing the gun at* NELSON.)

ANIBAL: Celestina. Could you please put that away—it's fine....

CELESTINA: Who is he?

ANIBAL: —this is my brother—Nelson—this is Nelson, it's okay....

(CELESTINA *reluctantly puts the gun in a pocket. Both men are greatly relieved.* NELSON *laughs nervously.*)

NELSON: Whoa. Fuckme. I love L A!

ANIBAL: I didn't know you were armed, Celestina. Christ.

CELESTINA: I stole it from the trucker while he was sleeping.

NELSON: Whoa.

ANIBAL: *(Still shaken)* Jesus.

CELESTINA: I'm sorry, Anibal, I....

ANIBAL: It's cool. It's just—*coño*. Heart attack.

CELESTINA: I wanted to protect you.

NELSON: *(To* ANIBAL*)* She wanted to protect you, asshole!

ANIBAL: *(To* NELSON*)* I'm not crazy about guns.

NELSON: *(To* CELESTINA*)* I am. *(Sotto to* ANIBAL.*)* She's gorgeous, man. Introduce.

ANIBAL: *(Wary)* Fuck. Nelson, this is Celestina. Celestina, this is my little brother, Nelson.

(CELESTINA *goes to shake* NELSON's *hand.)*

CELESTINA: *(To* NELSON*)* Nice to meet you.

NELSON: *(Big charming smile)* So Celestina, what's up?!

ANIBAL: *(Sotto to* NELSON*)* Nelson...slow....

NELSON: *(Sotto to* ANIBAL*)* Step back or I'll bodyslam you....

ANIBAL: *(Sotto to* NELSON*; re:* CELESTINA*)* ...disturbed...?

NELSON: *(To* CELESTINA*)* ...I'm married, okay? But. I'm separated from my wife. Bitch left me. Got drunk one night, said: "You know, Nelson, deep inside o' my heart, I just don't like you fucking little greasy Puerto Ricans!" I said, "fuck you, ho'" and threw a hand grenade at her.

CELESTINA: *(Amused)* You threw a hand grenade...?

ANIBAL: *(Horrified)* You threw a hand grenade...?

NELSON: *(Defensive)* It didn't go off! We filed for divorce. That little baby got a father?

CELESTINA: I'm looking for him. His name is Rodrigo Cruz.

NELSON: You married to him?

CELESTINA: No but I'm going to make him!

NELSON: You love this man?

CELESTINA: I don't know.

NELSON: Well, if you don't find him, let me know. I love children. I understand children. You have beautiful eyes, Celestina.

CELESTINA: Thank you.

ANIBAL: I may vomit.

NELSON: I can't stay too long, Celestina. I'm serving our country in the armed forces of the U S. Protecting us from...uhm...not communists...uhm...illegal aliens, drug king pins, and Arabs. It's dangerous work. My life is on the line each and every day. But I'm good to go! And the thing is, I gotta be back in Death Valley tonight—Death Valley, so appropriate, huh?—I have very important meetings with high ranking officers— then I go to Fort Benning, Georgia, Monday to finalize my divorce from my cracker wife. And then, in about two years, I'll be getting my discharge from the army. What I'm saying is...I won't be back this way for awhile. But I'm gonna come back in two years and look you up, okay? And if you ain't found that baby's father, I just might ask you to marry me, 'cause no woman should raise her baby alone. You understand? This cool with you, Celestina? Can I ask you?

CELESTINA: (Not knowing what to say) Uhm. You can ask me.

NELSON: Yes! Good! Well, my work is done here. Bye.

(NELSON goes to his raincoat and starts putting it on.)

ANIBAL: What do you mean? What are you doing?

NELSON: I gotta get back to Death Valley. Duty calls.

ANIBAL: Right now? Stay and eat with us.

NELSON: (Looking at his watch) No! My watch died! Fuckit. Yes. I gotta go. I'll take my dump on the road. I'm fucked I'm not there.

ANIBAL: This is happening too fast—.

NELSON: What's life? A fucking blink. Get used to it. And thanks for introducing me to the woman of my dreams, homeboy.

(CELESTINA smiles. Then she gets another pain in her belly.)

CELESTINA: Ohhhhhhhh.

(NELSON *and* ANIBAL *quickly go to* CELESTINA.)

ANIBAL & NELSON: You okay??

CELESTINA: *(Still in pain)* It's okay. Thank you. *(Another jolt)* Why is my baby doing this? Why is he tapping my spine with his fingers? What code is that? What words?

(NELSON *looks at her pregnant stomach.*)

NELSON: May I?

(CELESTINA *nods yes and* NELSON *kneels at her feet and rubs her belly. The pain slowly subsides.* CELESTINA *smiles with relief.*)

CELESTINA: Thank you, Nelson.

(NELSON *puts his head on her stomach, listening to the sounds inside.*)

NELSON: Check it out. I can hear the ocean! Stars being scraped across the sky!

CELESTINA: *(Delighted)* You can?

NELSON: I hear a little body searching for the way out. Little bones. *(To her stomach.)* Yo in there. I'mma wait for you, little man. Be the father of your dreams. You come outta this deep night you're in, *hijo de mi alma*, see my big-ass smile, you're gonna know what sunshine is! That cool? And you tell your beautiful mami to wait for me, okay *mijo*?

(NELSON *kisses* CELESTINA'S *stomach. Moved,* CELESTINA *gently kisses the top of* NELSON'S *head.*)

(NELSON *gets up.* NELSON *and* ANIBAL *have a long embrace.*)

ANIBAL: Six years, Nelson. Six fucking years.

NELSON: This is the happiest night of my life!

(NELSON *opens the door. Sirens. He disappears into the rain.* ANIBAL *goes to the door.*)

ANIBAL: You'll never get to Death Valley in that rain....

NELSON: *(Off)* A man would!

(ANIBAL *watches* NELSON *driving away, his back to the audience.* ANIBAL *sadly waves goodbye.* CELESTINA *looks at* ANIBAL.)

(ANIBAL *closes the door. Sirens stop.*)

(CELESTINA *is watching* ANIBAL *who is quiet a long moment, his mind far away.*)

CELESTINA: You okay?

(*Beat. He tries to smile. He starts clearing up the kitchen table.*)

ANIBAL: Are you really going to wait for him? Two years?

CELESTINA: I don't know what "two years" means, Anibal.

(ANIBAL *rubs his tired eyes—then look at his watch—then realizes it's not working.*)

ANIBAL: I don't even know what time it is. It could be next week. I don't remember this morning. I don't remember kissing Debbie goodbye or working or eating or driving from L A X or finding a hitchhiker in the storm of the century. And was my fucking little brother really here? I can't believe he's a man already! Ten minutes ago, I was bodyslamming him!

CELESTINA: Why don't we eat?

ANIBAL: *(Trying to focus)* Eat. Yeah. Eat.

(ANIBAL *and* CELESTINA *sit at the kitchen table.* CELESTINA *can hardly wait and immediately stuffs her mouth with food, eating with the passion of a starving person.*)

CELESTINA: *(Mouth full)* This is the best food!

ANIBAL: *(Concerned)* Easy...Celestina...easy....

(ANIBAL and CELESTINA continue their dinner. This should take it's natural time—despite the speed with which CELESTINA attacks her food—and should happen in silence.)

(All the while ANIBAL and CELESTINA may make periodic eye contact—smile—look away—sometimes ANIBAL finds himself staring—sometimes CELESTINA does.)

(Suddenly the house is rocked by several claps of harsh thunder. The lightning outside lights up the house through the windows brighter than could possibly occur in nature.)

(CELESTINA looks at ANIBAL.)

CELESTINA: *Me pregunto...me pregunto como sera haberte amado en cada etapa de tu vida, Anibal.*

(Beat. ANIBAL looks at CELESTINA and she continues in Spanish.)

CELESTINA: *Amar al ninito que fuiste, y tomarte de la mano, y ayudarte a cruzar la calle, y besar tu barriguita gordita de bebe, y peinar tus grenitas de chiquillo. Y luego, mas adelante, amar al anciano en que te convertiste, y besar tus arrugas profundas, y suavizar tu pelo canoso, y deleitar tu sabio y cansado corazon, y mirar fijamente hacia adentro de esos ojos misteriosos, mas alla de las cataratas, y muy adentro de ti, hacia los verdes prados donde uno nunca envejece. No te pareceria lindo tener ese tipo de amor, Anibal? El amor de toda una vida?*

(Beat. ANIBAL smiles nervously.)

ANIBAL: What?

CELESTINA: What?

ANIBAL: I didn't know you could speak Spanish.

CELESTINA: *(Smiles) Solamente hablo Espanol cuando estoy enamorada.*

ANIBAL: What?

(Beat)

CELESTINA: Don't you speak any Spanish?

ANIBAL: *(Sad)* I don't.

CELESTINA: You don't?

ANIBAL: I don't.

CELESTINA: Why not?

ANIBAL: Sometimes...I don't know...you forget things...

CELESTINA: But how do you forget a language?

ANIBAL: I happened, Celestina. It's not nice and I'm not proud of it, but it happened.

CELESTINA: I'm sorry.

ANIBAL: All I know is "*coño!*"

CELESTINA: *(Laughs)* Well, "*coño*"'s useful.

(CELESTINA laughs sadly. ANIBAL laughs with her. He looks at her. She reaches out a hand. He takes it and holds it a moment.)

ANIBAL: *(Pulling away)* I'll get the sofabed ready for you.

CELESTINA: *(Beat)* Okay. I'll help you set up.

(During the following, ANIBAL goes to the sofabed, pulls it out. He goes to the closet and comes back with pillows, blankets, and sheets. Together he and CELESTINA make the sofabed. If necessary for timing, ANIBAL could go through whatever bedtime ritual he needs: turning off lights, locking the door, turning on the security system, taking out the trash, etc.)

(Toward the end of the speech, while ANIBAL is deeper in his memories, he stops looking at CELESTINA. Behind ANIBAL, facing upstage, CELESTINA takes off her maternity dress and slips into a nightgown she keeps in her shopping bag.)

She lets her long hair down. She looks more unearthly, more angelic than ever.)

ANIBAL: I made love with Debbie just last night. Or was it this morning? *(Beat)* I had to talk her into spending the night, instead of sleeping in her office again. It seems like a million years ago. *(Beat)* I know Debbie from high school in the Bronx. We went out. Then she went out of state for college and I couldn't afford college so I stayed behind and worked. She married her English professor and moved to Ohio. I wanted to kill myself. I spent the next five years getting into these other relationships. The first one, I was twenty-two. The woman I fell in love with was thirty-nine. We had a great time together. But I took her home to meet my parents and my father made a pass at her and it was over. Then I fell in love with a blonde. She was a real beauty. But she came from this fucked up home and she had a drug problem and she drank too much and the night I told her I didn't love her anymore she tried to throw herself out of a moving car on the Belt Parkway. Then I fell in love with a series of lesbians. Every woman I liked turned out to be gay! Then one night, New Year's Eve, I'm living in the Lower East Side, the phone rings, it's Debbie. She left her husband. She left Ohio. She was staying at her sister's in Harlem. Would I like to get together. I said sure. *(Beat)* I went to her place. I didn't know what to expect. She was staying in one of those worn out tenements with the steam heat up too high and the steel radiators that clamored all night, and Willie Colon and laughing and partying and loud kissing coming at you from all the apartments all over us. People just exploding! Going nuts! I remember the smell of *tos—tos—*.

CELESTINA: *Tostones!*

ANIBAL: Tostones! And rice and beans and garlic and oregano and *lechon—lechon—*.

CELESTINA: *Lechon asado!*

ANIBAL: *Lechon asado!* You know: everything cooked
with a lot of *man*—.

CELESTINA: *Manteca!*

ANIBAL: *Manteca!* And I held Debbie all night long.
We didn't fuck. I kissed her a lot. We touched all over.
But we didn't go to bed. We were starting over. I was
figuring out this new body. She seemed richer. All the
years we hadn't seen each other, miles she's traveled,
all this married wisdom and experience she had that
I didn't have. I felt like a boy, a child, in the arms of
this mature woman. We decided that night to go to
Los Angeles together and start over. Be in that one city
where you can really re-make yourself. Pan for gold in
the L A River. She wanted to get rich on the movies. I
wanted to get away from the racists who thought of me
only as a spik. *(Beat)* As we were holding each other,
touching each other, I started to remember something
I thought I had forgotten. It was when I was a little
boy. I don't even remember how old. We were living
in Newark, New Jersey. We were visiting my cousins
who lived in a big house in Patchogue, Long Island.
My child's memory makes that house enormous, like
a Victorian haunted house, but maybe it wasn't. They
had thirteen kids. We used to watch *lucha libre* together,
professional wrestling, all the time. One night, after a
party, my cousin Cheo told me how he could feel his
balls flapping around in his pants when he danced to
American music. His balls went flap-flap-flap when he
danced to rock-n-roll. Cheo taught me about exponents
and square roots. He went to Vietnam. *(Beat)* One
night I was on the second floor of my cousins' house. I
remember walking past a dark bedroom: the door was
open. I thought I heard a voice inside calling my name.
I went in. My cousin Eva was there. She was older than
me. I remember her standing by the window. I could

see her face lit up by a streetlight—or was it the moon?
I remember there was a heavy smell in the room. And I
don't know how I eventually got there...but I ended up
lying in bed with Eva. I was on my back, looking at the
ceiling. Eva was kneeling next to me. Then Eva lifted
her dress and she was straddling me and pressing her
pelvis into me. I think she had her underwear on. I had
my pants on and I didn't know why she was doing
this to me, though I knew I had to do this because she
was my older cousin, therefore she had authority. I
remember her legs being smooth. I remember her face.
She was looking out the window. I don't remember
how long this lasted. I don't remember if anyone came
in. I don't remember if anyone ever knew about this,
though, later on it seemed that everybody knew. I liked
Eva on top of me. I remember her weight. I liked her
weight. I don't remember if I got hard or not: I was
only a little boy! I liked watching Eva's face, the way
she looked out the window. How the light struck half
her face. I wish I could remember her mouth! I think
it was open. But I don't remember. Was there a smile?
Did she bite her lower lip? Was she talking to me? Did
she say something in Spanish? I remember her eyes.
(Beat) So I fell in love with Eva. She was all I thought
about. And I think my mother suspected something
and she was worried about us, though first cousins
had married several times in my family. One night my
mother and I were washing dishes together, side-by-
side. And we had the only conversation about sex we
were ever to have. Without looking at me, she said:
"Anibal, remember: there is some fruit you are not
allowed to eat." And that's all she said. And I knew
exactly what she meant. And it was all she had to say
to me. *(Beat)* I've never forgotten Eva. Even in Debbie's
arms after five years of missing her and wanting her,
I thought easily of Eva. It's like...the space around my
body was permanently curved—or dented—by Eva's

heaviness. I wonder if love sometimes does that to you. It alters the physics around you in some way: changing the speed of light and the shape of space and how you experience time.

CELESTINA: What do you think made you fall in love with those women?

ANIBAL: Do you think I know?

(ANIBAL *turns around to look at* CELESTINA *who has changed into her nightgown. She smiles at him.*)

(Beat)

CELESTINA: Would you rub my feet?

ANIBAL: What?

CELESTINA: Would you rub my feet? They're freezing.

(Beat)

ANIBAL: Uhm, sure.

(Beat)

(CELESTINA *sits on the sofabed and puts her bare feet up expectantly.* ANIBAL *sits with her, her feet on his lap. He gently rubs her feet. She closes her eyes in bliss.*)

CELESTINA: Hmmmmmm...yeah....

(CELESTINA *seems to fall asleep, a look of peace and serenity on her face.* ANIBAL *looks at her a moment and can't help but smile.*)

ANIBAL: *Buenas noches.*

(ANIBAL *starts to get up.* CELESTINA *opens her eyes.*)

CELESTINA: Kiss my toes.

ANIBAL: ...What?

CELESTINA: Just once?

ANIBAL: Kiss your—what—?

CELESTINA: Please? Just once?

(Beat)

ANIBAL: Okay.

(ANIBAL kisses CELESTINA's toes one by one. She smiles with each little kiss, trying not to giggle, eyes still closed.)

(ANIBAL finishes and starts to leave.)

CELESTINA: No you don't.

ANIBAL: Now what?

CELESTINA: Higher.

ANIBAL: ...Higher?

CELESTINA: Up the body.

ANIBAL: Okay.

(ANIBAL kisses CELESTINA's knees. She sighs deeply, stretching out.)

CELESTINA: Little higher.

(ANIBAL kisses CELESTINA's thighs. She whispers.)

CELESTINA: Up.

(ANIBAL kisses CELESTINA's enormous stomach.)

CELESTINA: More up.

(ANIBAL kisses CELESTINA's breasts.)

CELESTINA: Keep going.

(ANIBAL kisses CELESTINA's neck.)

CELESTINA: ...Home, traveler. You're home!

(ANIBAL kisses CELESTINA lightly once on the lips. They hold each other a long moment. We hear the sound of the rain beating against the house. They don't look at each other as they talk.)

ANIBAL: I'm afraid.

CELESTINA: Don't be.

ANIBAL: Not about bodies. I'm afraid we're going to be mixing my sad dreams with your wild ones.

CELESTINA: *(Smiles)* Maybe they'll have beautiful children, Anibal.

(ANIBAL kisses her gently on the lips. She opens her mouth to him and takes him in, kissing him back with all the passion in her body.)

ANIBAL: Celestina.

(CELESTINA speaks to ANIBAL as she holds him.)

CELESTINA: I'm a stranger in my own body, Anibal. A stranger to my own past. My memories don't make sense to me. I doubt everything. I don't even believe what people verify for me. I even wonder if my real name is Celestina del Sol! *(Beat)* Sometimes you're with somebody and you don't seem so strange to yourself anymore. Somehow, by luck or chemistry or divine intervention or insanity, you collide with another life, and there's an explosion followed by peace. For a second, a year, fifty years—whatever those things mean—you feel you've reached some kind of home. Sometimes there's no "time" —only an endless now that needs to be filled with life. To be rescued from habit and death. *(Beat)* C'mon.

ANIBAL: Okay.

(ANIBAL takes CELESTINA's hand and leads her to the ladders which go up to the floating bed.)

(As they climb the ladders, the rest of the house seems to disappear and be replaced by vague twinkling stars and crescent moons and dark, silvery clouds.)

(As they reach the bed, there's another knock at the door.)

(The house instantly changes back to its normal state, like a spell broken. ANIBAL looks at the door.)

CELESTINA: *(Sotto)* Who's that?

ANIBAL: *(Sotto)* Stay.

(ANIBAL climbs down the ladder. CELESTINA stays up on the bed.)

(He opens the door. Sirens. He is surprised by the sight of hundreds of Sparkletts water bottles covering the porch.)

(NELSON is there. NELSON looks different. His hair is slightly longer. His moustache is gone. His army clothes have been replaced by blue jeans, sneakers, and an old jeans jacket. He walks with a cane.)

(But that's not the only thing that's changed. Something childlike and happy has been taken away from NELSON. Though he mouths some of the same old lines, they lack his spirit.)

ANIBAL: Nelson?

NELSON: *(Tired smile)* Brother!

(NELSON scoops up ANIBAL in a bear hug and pounds his back.)

ANIBAL: *(Confused)* What are you doing here?

(NELSON holds ANIBAL for a long time. ANIBAL has to pull away. NELSON won't let him.)

NELSON: Look at you! You get older and uglier all the time!

ANIBAL: Everything okay?

NELSON: Fucking just wanna hold you, man.

(ANIBAL, worried, pulls away from NELSON.)

ANIBAL: What happened? Couldn't you get back to Death Valley? Are the freeways closed?

NELSON: Death Valley? What are you talking about? Everything's great. Hey, I'm a free man! I can do whatever I want now!

ANIBAL: *(Noticing)* Hey, what happened to you? Why's your face like that?

(NELSON comes into the living room, closing the door behind him. Sirens stop. NELSON looks around.)

NELSON: Fuckme, the old place hasn't changed at all. Everything's just the way I remember it!

ANIBAL: Wait. Wait a minute. What happened to you? You look totally—why are your clothes like that?

NELSON: Jesus, will you get over my appearance? What are you, gay? I'm lucky to be alive, motherfucker. I need a beer. *(He goes to the refrigerator to get a beer.)*

ANIBAL: *(Still confused)* Have a beer.

NELSON: I was pissed at you, bro. I don't mind telling you. All my letters to you came back, your phone's been disconnected, I thought, "that asshole moved without telling me! He makes me drive cross country— three fucking days—and he's not there, I'mma kill him!"

(Beat)

ANIBAL: You've been driving three days?

NELSON: Hello? From Georgia? Have you gone stupid? You have no memory? What did I tell you two years ago? Soon's I get to Benning, get my discharge and my divorce from Mein Kampf, I was comin' back here, find that girl, and ask her to marry me.

(A short beat as ANIBAL looks at NELSON.)

ANIBAL: Two years? Nelson are you drunk? That was only a few minutes ago you left here and said that.

NELSON: *(Laughs)* You gotta get outta L A, bro. Your brain!

ANIBAL: A half hour—

NELSON: Maybe to you! Mister Lalaland! You still got on the same boring clothes you had that night! And wasn't it raining then?

ANIBAL: *(Nervous, worried)* Cut the shit, Nelson...

NELSON: You cut the shit or I'll bodyslam you! Where's Celestina? You hiding her? Did she have her baby? Does the baby know who I am? Does he ask about me? I bet he loves me!

ANIBAL: *(Trying to focus)* She...she uh....

NELSON: And you! You fuck! Why did all my letters come back? You think it was fun being out in fucking Bosnia and not hearing from you all that fucking time!? Fuck you!

ANIBAL: Bosnia?

NELSON: Yo, the war? The Battle of Mostar? Are you stoned or what? Don't they get the news in L A? *(He reaches into his raincoat and pulls up a handful of medals. He throws them across the room, one-by-one.)* R-com with two oak leaf clusters! Army Achievement Medal! Bronze Star with three oak leaf clusters! Silver star with two oak leaf clusters! Bosnia Liberation Medal!

(NELSON laughs and digs into another pocket and pulls out a dozen letters he wrote to ANIBAL, all of which were returned to him. ANIBAL looks with amazement at their postmarks.)

ANIBAL: These letters are from Bosnia.

NELSON: Beautiful land. I met a pregnant girl, too. Man, I really wanted to marry her—broke my heart to leave her—but "no," I said, "I have the most beautiful girl named Celestina waiting for me in the States!"

(ANIBAL, shaking, puts the letters down.)

ANIBAL: How can one night be two years...Celestina...?

(CELESTINA *sits up in the bed and climbs down the ladder to the living room during the following:*)

NELSON: They had to fucking put me in a fucking army hospital 'cause I have a fucking nervous breakdown? I thought: I gotta live through this so I can see my bride and my child again! And I said this to myself, Anibal, over and over, like a prayer, and you know that was the only thing that kept some fucking Serbian sniper bullet from finding the back of my head or some landmine from erasing my legs. The unbearable luck of her name!

(CELESTINA *is in the living room.* NELSON *turns to face her. He can't believe what he sees.*)

CELESTINA: Hi Nelson.

(*A long pause as* NELSON *just takes her in and smiles.*)

NELSON: Hey.

CELESTINA: How are you?

NELSON: That's really you.

CELESTINA: It's really me.

NELSON: (*Answering her question*) I'm a little tired. Ass hurts from driving three days from Georgia!

(NELSON *starts to cry.* CELESTINA *goes to him.*)

CELESTINA: Hey, hey, what is it?

NELSON: Nothing. It's nothing. No problem.

(CELESTINA *wipes* NELSON's *eyes.*)

CELESTINA: I heard what happened to you in the war. I'm really sorry.

NELSON: It's over. I lived. I'm gonna forget it as soon as I can.

CELESTINA: (*Touching her stomach*) I have a lot to tell you...as you can see....

NELSON: Oh yeah! Uh-huh! I can see a lot has happened in your life, Celestina!

ANIBAL: *(To* CELESTINA*)* Do you know what's going on here?

CELESTINA: *(Torn)* Don't be afraid, Anibal, please...

NELSON: *(Not listening)* But what's weird? I'm looking at you. It's like you never aged a day!

CELESTINA: That's because I haven't!

NELSON: And you're pregnant again. Just like that night!

CELESTINA: It's not—Nelson—that's what I have to tell you—and you know I'd only tell you the truth. You left Los Angeles. You went to war...but here, in this house, time didn't pass; it's still the same night; you left a little while ago. And this baby...it's Rodrigo's baby...do you understand that...?

NELSON: *(Laughs)* Fuck you!

CELESTINA: It's the truth!

NELSON: I can't believe you would lie to me!

CELESTINA: And Anibal—two years have passed—whether you want to believe it or not!

ANIBAL: How is that possible?

CELESTINA: It's me, Anibal. I've infected you! I've changed the "time" around you—.

ANIBAL: But—who's been paying the light bill?! Who's been paying the rent?! Where's Debbie been?! What happened to my job?!

NELSON: What the fuck are you two trying to do to me?!

CELESTINA: *(To both men)* Things have happened....

NELSON: *(Overlapping with* CELESTINA*)* Look, I know that's Anibal's baby! Okay?! I can see what happened!

CELESTINA: Nothing happened!

NELSON: You two fell in love! It's cool! And I guess we didn't make any promises to each other, huh Celestina?

CELESTINA: I'm sorry, Nelson....

NELSON: So I just want to see that little baby before I go! Where is he? Where's that little boy I talked to? Did something happen to him?!

CELESTINA: He hasn't been born—!

NELSON: *(Angry)* Man, I don't need to hear this doubletalk BULLSHIT any more! Fuck you both! I don't give a fuck if you two fell in love with each other! I was stupid to think you would wait for me! But you didn't! You didn't wait for me, did you!?

*(*NELSON *makes a move toward* CELESTINA. ANIBAL *tries to protect her.)*

*(*NELSON *grabs* ANIBAL, *lifts him up, and bodyslams him into the floor.)*

*(*CELESTINA *goes to* ANIBAL *and holds him.* ANIBAL *writhes in pain, speechless.* NELSON *is breathing hard, instantly sorry he hurt his brother.)*

(Silence)

*(*NELSON *quietly cries.)*

ANIBAL: *(In pain)* Oh my God.

NELSON: I'm sorry, bro. I'm not myself. Something in myself got taken out sometime as I was looking through the sights of the tank, lining up targets, watching things blow up. Jesus shit! I got so much I gotta forget!

ANIBAL: Jesus Christ, bro....

(NELSON *goes to* ANIBAL, *lifts him, and puts him gently on the sofabed. He holds* ANIBAL.)

NELSON: I'm sorry, bro, you know I fucking love you, man! I'm a total asshole! I shouldn't have come here! You got something good with your woman, man, that's cool, that's great! I gotta step aside and let your happiness be, man! Fuck me! I'm sorry! You're my fucking brother and I'm sorry!

ANIBAL: Nelson....

(NELSON *wipes his eyes and goes to the door. He opens it. Sirens*)

(NELSON *runs out into the night.*)

ANIBAL: Nelson? Nelson!

(ANIBAL *gets up to follow* NELSON.)

CELESTINA: Anibal—don't leave me alone!

(ANIBAL *goes to the door.*)

ANIBAL: I gotta talk to him!

(ANIBAL *runs out into the night to chase down* NELSON, *closing the door behind him.*)

(CELESTINA *is alone.*)

(*She goes to the door and waits for* ANIBAL. *She closes the door. She opens it again. She closes it again. She sits.*)

(*In moments she has no idea how much time has passed since* ANIBAL *left. For all she knows it could be days, weeks later. She's getting more and more nervous. Nervousness gives way to panic. She shakes. She looks around.*)

(*Unable to bear the pain of waiting any longer,* CELESTINA *gets quickly dressed. She puts on her shoes and* ANIBAL'*s suede jacket. She goes to the door.*)

(CELESTINA *runs out into the night, leaving the door open.*)

(The digital clocks stop blinking and a new time comes on: 8:06.)

(ANIBAL comes in. He's got his arm around NELSON, who is soaking wet and looks disheveled. ANIBAL helps NELSON sit. NELSON sits with his face in his hands.)

(ANIBAL closes the door behind him. Sirens stop. She looks very shaken.)

ANIBAL: *(To NELSON)* ...it's okay...it's okay, bro...you're home....

NELSON: Thanks, man.

ANIBAL: Celestina! I found him! Bet you thought we'd never get back! Took all night but I got him! *(No answer. He goes to the offstage bathroom.)* Celestina? *(No response. He goes back to the living room.)* Celestina!

NELSON: Celestina!

ANIBAL: Goddammit.

NELSON: Where is she?

ANIBAL: Her shoes are gone...the jacket...all the clocks are going...she's taken off...shit! ...Stay here.... *(He grabs a coat, and runs out into the rain. From offstage:)* Celestina!

(The door closes with a SLAM! NELSON is left alone on stage. Lights start to go down on him.)

NELSON: Celestina.

(Lights to black. The sound of the rain stops. NELSON calls out in the dark, silent house.)

NELSON: Celestina!

(Black out)

END OF CLOUD TECTONICS

EPILOGUE

(In the dark, the bolero from the Prologue starts again, though quieter, distorted if possible. Lights come up downstage.)

(During CELESTINA's *speech, the crew comes on and disassembles the house. By the end of* CELESTINA's *speech, there should be nothing left of* ANIBAL's *house in Echo Park.)*

(The ladders next to the bed are removed and the bed is lowered to the stage.)

(The glass wall is removed from the house and left free-standing, to the side. Water drips down the side of the glass wall, as in the Prologue.)

(A microphone on a C-stand is placed downcenter.)

(It's forty years later.)

*(*CELESTINA *enters and goes to the microphone. She's no longer pregnant. Her clothes are nicer than before. But otherwise she looks the same. She could be wearing a slightly futuristic costume. She's pushing a stroller. She wears* ANIBAL's *aged suede jacket.)*

(She's talking to the baby. She's in mid-conversation.)

CELESTINA: Can you believe this rain for L A? *Coño!* *(Beat)* The last time I was here it was raining just like this, right before you were born, and Los Angeles has changed so much, *mijo.* I can't get over it. The Big One was finally born—a monster with seven epicenters—

releasing unimaginable waves of energy and killing
many unprepared people—the six active oil fields on
Pico exploded—glass came down from the towers in
Downtown and Century City and Burbank like floating
guillotines—there were fourteen million refugees—
and Los Angeles died for a while. People went back to
New York and the Midwest. There was a long sleep.
(Beat) But people came back. They came back for the
things they loved about L A the first time. They rebuilt
the city. And the city was reborn—and now it's better
than ever! Look, *mijo,* you see? That building over
there? That's the White House. They moved it from
Washington D C and put it on Wilshire Blvd. And
there's the United Nations building. All of it is here
in the new L A. The new capitol of the United States.
The capitol of world culture and trade. The capitol
of the Third World. Boy, they really fixed this place
up, Anibal! The largest subway system in the world
is here, connecting everything from Catalina Island
to the Angeles National Forest. The air is clean! It's
chic to read! All the street signs are in Spanish! They
integrated all the neighborhoods! There are no more
poor sections! No more big earthquakes for another
one hundred and fifty years! In L A, that's forever!

*(The house has been completely dismantled and removed
from the stage. It looks like the opening of the play. The
bolero ends or fades out.)*

(In the dark, ANIBAL *enters and lies on the bed.)*

*(*CELESTINA *pushes the stroller to the bed.)*

(Lights on the bed go up. We can see clearly that ANIBAL *is
an old man in his seventies.* ANIBAL *lies in bed, reading a
book.)*

*(The light around the bed goes very dark, leaving the bed in
limbo. The vague twinkling stars, crescent moons, and dark,*

silvery clouds of the earlier scene return: it should seem as if once again the bed were floating in space.)

*(*CELESTINA *goes to* ANIBAL'*s side and she looks at him a long moment.)*

CELESTINA: *(Big smile)* Is that really you, Anibal?

ANIBAL: *(Looking up from his book)* Huh?

CELESTINA: It's me, Anibal! I'm back! I just got into L A! I didn't think I'd remember how to get to Echo Park—but that bus stop at Virgil and Santa Monica is still there—and your house is exactly the same—the earthquake didn't hurt it—I can't believe my luck!

*(*ANIBAL *looks at* CELESTINA *a long moment. He doesn't remember her.)*

ANIBAL: Are you the new nurse?

CELESTINA: It's me. It's Celestina! I'm back!

ANIBAL: You're not the new nurse? Who's going to give me a bath?

CELESTINA: ...I'm Celestina.

ANIBAL: Who is Celestina?

CELESTINA: Anibal, stop it.

ANIBAL: Who are you?

(Beat)

CELESTINA: Celestina del Sol.

*(*CELESTINA *waits for the name to click in* ANIBAL'*s memory. It doesn't.* ANIBAL *holds out his hand.)*

ANIBAL: I'm Anibal de la Luna. Nice to meet you.

(Disappointed, CELESTINA *shakes hands with* ANIBAL.*)*

CELESTINA: Nice to meet you.

ANIBAL: Are you here for the house? It's a craftsman. Built in the last century. In the 1915.

CELESTINA: Don't you remember me?

ANIBAL: Well, I'm sorry. I'm afraid I don't.

CELESTINA: C'mon, Anibal, think, you have to remember.

ANIBAL: When did we meet?

CELESTINA: I think it was forty years ago, but I can't be sure.

ANIBAL: Forty years! *Coño!* Memory doesn't go back that far!

CELESTINA: It's just like yesterday for me! You picked me up by the side of the road. I was pregnant. You took me to this house. We had quesadillas! You rubbed my feet!

ANIBAL: I did?

CELESTINA: I remember every moment of that night! I never stopped thinking about you! And I meant to come back sooner, but I just lost track of the "time"!

ANIBAL: It couldn't have been forty years ago. Eyesight isn't so hot—these damn cataracts, you know?—but— you're a kid. What're you, twenty-five? Twenty-six?

(Slight beat)

CELESTINA: I'm not really sure.

(This response seems to jog something in ANIBAL's memory, but he isn't sure what.)

ANIBAL: Well, if you're here for the house, make yourself at home, look around—it's a craftsman!

CELESTINA: I know it's a fucking craftsman, Anibal!

ANIBAL: *(Laughs; re: baby.)* And who's that little guy?

CELESTINA: My son. I think I was in labor with him for six months!

ANIBAL: Again, please?

CELESTINA: Never mind!

ANIBAL: How old is he?

CELESTINA: Do you think I know?

ANIBAL: Why do I feel like I've had this conversation before?

CELESTINA: His name is Anibal. Anibal del Sol y la Luna. His father's dead. Rodrigo's body was pulled out of the L A River in the storm of the century.

ANIBAL: *Coño!*

CELESTINA: It was the night that we met, Anibal. Your brother was in the army. You had a girlfriend named Debbie.

ANIBAL: Debbie? You're a week too late. We buried her last week in Anaheim. Disney did a fucking hell of a job burying my wife, let me tell you. Those people know how to throw a funeral! They are true merchants of death!

CELESTINA: So you married her, huh?

ANIBAL: Had to. Knocked her up.

CELESTINA: And Nelson?

ANIBAL: He's a war hero, you know. Lives up the street. Married a beautiful girl many years ago...a Bosnian. They have thirteen kids!

CELESTINA: *(Smiles)* Good.

(ANIBAL *stares a* CELESTINA *a long moment.*)

ANIBAL: You look...*coño*...you look so familiar. You look vaguely like...there was a young woman...on a night that seemed to last forever...she was...crazy...and very fat....

CELESTINA: I was pregnant!

ANIBAL: ...but it was some forty years ago...before the Big One...before they moved the capitol...something happened to me back then...I blacked out for a couple of years...nobody could explain it...I woke up and it was two years later! I had dreams in my coma that made no sense! *(Laughs)* But you know what? It was so long ago and so much has happened since then, so much life, so much dying, so many changes, it just gets buried under all the time between now and then, you know? It's like, somewhere in my mind is a ditch, a very dark and deep hole, and time keeps filling this hole with all the debris of my life, the details: every name, face, taste, sound: gone! Down the hole! Outta reach! *Coño!* What's the point of that, huh? Does that make any sense to you?

CELESTINA: No.

ANIBAL: No. You're very beautiful, though. Kind. It would be nice to remember you. To have been in love with you.

CELESTINA: We were in love, Anibal.

ANIBAL: How do you know we were in love?

CELESTINA: We lived together for two years, didn't we?

ANIBAL: We did?

CELESTINA: They were the happiest two years of my life.

ANIBAL: You sure it was me?

(Beat. CELESTINA wipes her tears, then reaches out, touches ANIBAL's hand, and kisses it.)

CELESTINA: I should probably let you get some sleep. It's been great seeing you again, Anibal.

ANIBAL: Yes.

CELESTINA: You take care of yourself, okay?

ANIBAL: Thanks for dropping by. Listen, this house is a steal at this price! Great place to raise a family!

CELESTINA: I'll keep that in mind.

ANIBAL: Yes. Good.

CELESTINA: Is there anything I can do for you before I go?

(Beat)

ANIBAL: Yes there is.

CELESTINA: What?

ANIBAL: Would you rub my feet? They're freezing.

(Beat)

CELESTINA: *(Smiles)* Okay.

(CELESTINA gets into bed with ANIBAL. He puts his feet up on her lap. She rubs his feet gently.)

(The feeling of her hands on his feet has an instant and electrifying effect on ANIBAL. When he talks, he sounds like a young man again.)

ANIBAL: I searched Los Angeles for days and days after she left me. I went to that bus stop on the corner of Virgil and Santa Monica and waited there day and night. I called every hospital and went to every police station in L A County. *(Beat)* I imagined finding her. Living with her forever. I imagined long moments of silence between us when we didn't have anything to say. I imagined enduring the terror of a Los Angeles gone out of control because these quiet moments would be like iron wings and we'd be sheltered inside them. We wouldn't hear the noise of the earthquakes or the screams of a dying culture. But she never came back to me. I never saw her again. All I kept were memories of that extraordinary woman and a night that had that dream feeling to it, you know that feeling: there's a sound like suspended music,

air that doesn't move, time that doesn't add to itself.
It took me years but I finally understood that I had
encountered a true mystery that night, that I had taken
a living miracle into my house. That Celestina del Sol
was from a world I would never understand. That
sometimes Nature improvises. That Nature created a
woman that lived outside the field of time and may
never die. That someday everyone who ever knew her
and remembered her would be gone. That she would
live forever in that physical perfection like some kind
of exiled and forgotten goddess. And that trying to
understand such a life, and why love matters to it, why
a god would need to be loved too, was like trying to
understand the anatomy of the wind or the architecture
of silence or cloud tectonics. *(He laughs.)* Yeah. What
better way to respond to a miracle than to fall in love
with it?

*(During the following, lights start to go down on the bed.
The sound of the rain comes up.)*

ANIBAL: And at one point in the evening, I heard the
sound of Spanish, as love assumed the language my
parents spoke the night I was conceived, the language I
had forgotten....

(CELESTINA kisses ANIBAL.)

*(CELESTINA leaves the bed, takes the baby out of the stroller,
and starts walking to the bus stop with the baby in her
arms.)*

ANIBAL: Celestina said to me: *"Me pregunto como sera
haberte amado en cada etapa de tu vida, Anibal..."*

*(ANIBAL continues the speech in Spanish, quietly,
underneath CELESTINA's simultaneous, and louder,
translation:)*

CELESTINA: *(To the baby)* ... I wonder what it would
be like to love you in every age of your life, Anibal.

To love the little boy you were, and hold your hand,
and lead you across the street, and kiss your fat little
baby stomach, and comb your little boy's hair. And
then, later, to love the old man you've become, and
kiss your deep wrinkles, and smooth out the grey hair,
and delight your wise and tired heart, and stare into
those mysterious eyes, past the cataracts, and deep
into you, to the green landscapes where you never age.
Wouldn't it be sweet to have that kind of love, Anibal?

ANIBAL: "... *El amor de toda una vida.*"

(CELESTINA *has reached the bus stop with the baby.*)

CELESTINA: ...The love of a lifetime.

(ANIBAL *smiles sadly at the sweet memory. Then he forgets
it again and goes back to his book as if nothing happened.*)

(*Lights slowly to black on the bed.*)

(*At the dark bus stop,* CELESTINA *holds her thumb up,
hoping to catch a ride out of Los Angeles.*)

(*She reaches into a pocket and pulls out saltine crackers. She
gives one to the baby and eats the other.*)

(*Rain. Headlights. Blackout*)

END OF PLAY